Grow Your Gardening Business

From the Ground Up

Marie Glover

Disclaimer

This book contains information that is intended to help the readers be better informed consumers of health care. It is presented as general advice on health care. Always consult your doctor for your individual needs.

Before beginning any new exercise program, it is recommended that you seek medical advice from your personal physician.

This book is not intended to be a substitute for the medical advice of a licensed physician. The reader should consult with their doctor in any matters relating to his/her health.

This book is dedicated to Andrew Thorowgood. He approached me in 2020 for advice and encouragement on how to start a gardening business. I inspired him to take the plunge and he unknowingly became the inspiration for me writing this book. So, we have both helped each other.

Preface

This book is aimed at the person who maybe fed up with their current occupation and is thinking of changing careers to become a professional gardener. Or the young person fresh out of college and finding it difficult to get into the working world.

Through my 8 years of experience of trading as a gardener, plus many years before that as my main hobby and passion, I will guide you through the aspects you will need to consider when setting up a new business.

I have another business, Natural Therapy, doing private therapies such as massage, reflexology and hypnotherapy. I have been working self-employed since 2000, so I have plenty of experience.

I will highlight the positives and the challenges involved in going self-employed, suggesting ways round the challenges to enable making the decision process of taking that big step a little easier for you.

Although I am U.K based and information is based on services in the U.K, the general concept and ideas discussed in this book will be beneficial where ever you live.

In chapter 1 we will look at you, the skills and attributes that you have that will make gardening an appropriate occupation for you.

Chapter 2 we will look at some of the additional professional support that I have used over the past 8 years, that have enabled me to do a thorough job.

Chapter 3 I will list all the tools that I use to complete my maintenance gardening work. You may be pleased to see that you have a lot of them already and may result in less outlay for the start- up than you think.

Chapter 4 we will look at the different arenas of potential work that you could work in. There may be more than you think and hopefully this chapter will expand your mind of possibilities of work.

Chapter 5 we will debate the need for formal training in order to start working as a gardener. There are no set rules for this, it all comes down to personal preference.

Chapter 6 we will look at money, from how much to charge for your hourly rate and other matters, such as cost of insurance.

Chapter 7 we will look at the many different avenues for advertising your new business, even some ways that are free or cost very little.

Chapter 8 will list all the things you need to consider when looking at a new garden. It can be a bit daunting going into a new garden in the early days, but with the check list of questions I list, you will be more prepared to do a thorough initial assessment.

Chapter 9. We will look at what makes for good customer care and what attitudes of work you need to build a solid foundation of professional work.

Chapter 10 will lay out a plan of potential seasonal work to take you through the year. There are tasks that can be done in the dead of winter, it's not just a spring to autumn occupation.

Chapter 11 is in my view the most important chapter and one that makes this book different from all the other books on the market of setting up a gardening business. I will guide you through essential body care, drawing on my 30 years of experience of being an Occupational therapist, a massage therapist and from my interest in yoga. The exercises and advice I offer in this chapter will go a long way to ensuring you are fit for work. Gardening is a physically demanding job, you need to be in good physical health to do the work on a daily basis.

Chapter 12 will be a general discussion of topics, items and thoughts to consider around the idea of becoming a gardener.

It is hoped that you will enjoy this step by step guide book full of helpful tips and guidance to set you on the road to starting your own gardening business. While reading this book you will understand your own skills, strengths, and attributes and to use them to help you get started – no matter where you are now.

If you love the idea of working outside in the fresh air surrounded by nature appeals to you, then this is the book for you.

So, by the end of reading this book, you will be as prepared as much as possible to get your new business of to a flying start.

Table of Contents

Introduction

This book was written during the time of the Corona Virus outbreak of 2020; a year I bet many of us won't forget in a hurry! It was a time of worldwide upheaval, of immense uncertainty and changes forced upon us totally out of the blue. It was a time that many people found themselves unexpectedly unemployed, as many businesses folded or had to operate in different ways that restricted the number of people allowed in a space.

It was an unexpected chance to step off the daily tread mill and rat race of work and school runs that so many of us find ourselves in. It was a time of reflection and review. Friends of mine decided not to go back to their regular jobs, but to do work and interests that they had put off. Maybe you were in the same situation?

Did the time off give you chance to reflect on what you really want to do for work? Let's be truthful, work occupies a huge percentage of our time, so we need to be happy in our work, as time on this planet is limited.

Did the thought of being stuck in an office environment feel like a lump in your stomach, after the freedom of being at home for a few months, with the opportunity to go for a daily walk. The weather was exceptionally sunny and glorious in the UK and was calling us to be outside.

It was a time that people found solace in being in their garden, if they were fortunate to have one. It was a time that people found themselves growing vegetables, for maybe the first time, driven from an initial food shortage in the supermarkets from panic buying, but then from interest.

It was a time that people were allowed to follow their passion for gardening, as they now had time and great weather to be outdoors to connect with nature. So many people commented in the early days of the lock down, how loud the birds sounded; they hadn't had the time before to notice and while the world stood still, everything went quiet, except for nature, which thrived.

Gardening not only gave people something to do, it was a time to focus on a task, that for a time, took their minds off the worries of the world that were going on all around. It was a safety line for sanity.

Gardening gave hope for a better future, as seeds were sown with the promise of something good coming from it as a result further down the line. It also gave chance to be creative and to explore developing changes in the garden that people may have not had time to do before the crisis.

Nature had been there for us in a way many people discovered. My hope going into the future, is that we can now be there for nature. By becoming a professional gardener, you are doing your bit.

Your Big Why

Do you fancy becoming the next Monty Don?

So, maybe you know it's time for a change, but are standing at a crossroads unsure of what to do?

Maybe you are wondering if it's time to turn that hobby of gardening, which has become a personal passion, into a profitable career? 'They' say if you do a job you love, you never 'work' another day.

However, I accept that changing jobs is a huge decision and something you may be undecided on. So, in this book, I will talk you through all the positives and challenges that being a professional gardener brings. I have based this book on having been a professional gardener since 2012. So I'm talking from experience, to give you a realistic picture of what it entails, of all the positives and 'challenges' that I have encountered, so that you will gain a better understanding. So that if you do decide to 'go for it', you will go forward more prepared. The fact that you are reading this book already shows you're on the first step of heading for your goal.

Obviously everyone has their own issues and I may not have thought of every scenario, but I will give you a good overall picture to base a decision on.

Ok, let's take a moment out to focus on you.

I want you to take a few minutes to think of 3 reasons why you want to become a professional gardener. For example, "I want to work outside in the fresh air" or "I want to create lovely gardens" Don't spend too long on it, as these points should be from the heart.

1.

2.

3.

Next, I want you to write down 3 fears and worries that you may have at making this new start. For example, "will I earn enough money to sustain myself and my family?"

Sometimes getting fears out on paper and seeing them rationally helps to reduce the intensity of them mulling around in your head over and over.

1.

2.

3.

Now, the most important exercise. I want you to let your imagination go wild and think of 3 ways that this new exciting career will positively impact you and your family. For example, being self-employed will bring me greater freedom in my worklife.

1.

2.

3.

You will have, hopefully, finished the last exercise of Chapter 1 on a positive and have a good picture in your mind of the potential.

Ok, in Chapter One we have looked at you, why you want to become a professional gardener. You have listed some of your skills and what you hope to gain from this new work.

You may have surprised yourself at the skills, talents and attributes you have, that's great, but no one person has all the skills required for everything, otherwise you would be "Jack of all trades and master of none".

So, in the next chapter we will have a quick look at some of the help you can or may wish to draw upon to do a thorough job.

Professional Support

John Donne said in the 17th Century, "No man is an island". The same applies in the 21st Century.

So, following on from Chapter 1, I asked you to list some of your skills and attributes. I hope you could identify 5, if not more.

Even if you identified more than 5, the chances are you won't have all the skills required for every aspect of business.

Here is a list of some of the additional professional support I have used during the past 8 years of trading.

1. Accountant
2. Web designer
3. Tree Surgeon
4. Fellow Landscape gardener who was used to working on a larger scale than me, for some hard landscaping tasks in customer gardens
5. Machinery repair shop
6. Structural Engineer
7. Skip hire

8. Stone mason
9. Pest control

Have a think of anyone you know who has the skills/ business that you lack and how you could work together.

Tools for the Job

The saying "a bad work man blames his tools" has some merit.

From now on we will look at the practical aspects of gardening, starting with the basics of what tools you will need for the job and hopefully you will be positive after reading this chapter that you are closer to starting professional gardening than you think.

One of the daunting prospects of starting any new career is the 'start up' costs involved from starting from scratch.

But, the good news with gardening, is, I bet you already have a lot of the tools required already in your garage or shed. Ok they may need a bit of a dust down, a sharpen up and a bit of TLC, but you don't need the most expensive tools and gadgets to get started.

Let me list the tools I use on a regular basis, for you to see what tools you may already have and that you can tick off from the list.

1. A petrol mower.
2. A petrol strimmer
3. A hedge trimmer
4. A substantial weeding tool

5. Shears
6. Long handled loppers
7. Secateurs
8. Pruning saw
9. Ladder
10. Wood saw
11. Tape measure
12. Fork
13. Spade
14. Trowel
15. Lawn edging shears
16. Half Moon cutter
17. Broom
18. Dust pan and hand brush
19. A car/van that can hold it all, that will get dirty with soil and grass cuttings and become home to many snails and spiders.
20. A PH soil indicator.

It may seem obvious to mention using petrol tools, but I did start by using my electric mower for the first 2 years of trading. As long as the customer is happy for you to use their electricity and you have access to the socket with a long extension lead, there is nothing shameful in starting out initially using an electric mower.

However, I found an electric mower restrictive in lots of ways. A petrol mower gives you freedom and flexibility to be in any garden and not worry about having to gain access point to the socket. There is no long lead to get tangled up in and having to wind up at the end of the job. No power cuts to worry about and most importantly, no worry of mowing through the lead.

Ok, so we have established petrol is better, but which company to buy from?

Professional branding of tools is a personal choice, like clothing.

I can, however, recommend Mountfield for its mowers. It's an established company, with a range of mowers for a range of needs and budgets. Price starts at about £160 for a small basic mower, upwards to £400 - £500 for a top of the range model.

It's the brand that I have used for my past 2 mowers. I especially like that they do a small light weight mower than I can easily lift and place in the back of my car. You may possibly be doing on average 6 gardens a day. So that's 12 times a day you are lifting the mower in and out of your vehicle. You may be fine for the first few gardens, but as the working day progresses and you get tired, lifting a heavy mower may be the last thing you want to be doing. Care of your back is essential and will be discussed in Chapter 11.

But to summarize this chapter, we have looked at what tools you need for the job and briefly discussed the advantages of petrol tools, with a recommended supplier. The next chapter will look at all the different job titles of gardening where you use these tools.

WHAT AREAS COULD YOU WORK IN?

Ok, so you are thinking of becoming a professional gardener?

There are numerous avenues you could go down.

The first question I am asked when people know I'm a gardener is, "Are you a landscape gardener"?

This always makes me smile, as the term 'landscape gardener' has become a term, which to the public, epitomizes what a professional gardener is.

Yes, you could become a 'landscape gardener', but there are more options open to you.

But let's start with Landscape Gardener.

Landscape Gardener

A Landscape Gardener is someone who has good building skills and knowledge. The work focuses on creating the hard landscaping aspects of a garden, things such as:

1. laying a patio
2. laying a path
3. constructing a wall

4. constructing raised beds from wood
5. erecting a pergola or trellis
6. erecting or replacing fencing
7. erecting or replacing gates
8. building a pond
9. erecting a shed or greenhouse
10. removing or laying a new lawn

The list is not exhaustive but these tasks differentiate a 'landscape gardener' from the next category, a maintenance gardener.

Maintenance Gardener

A maintenance gardener could be involved in some of the tasks of the landscape gardener but their focus is more on the everyday jobs that keep a garden looking good. It is less 'building' orientated and more 'traditional' gardening. So it will include tasks such as:

1. Weeding paths and borders
2. Mowing a lawn
3. Treating a lawn by applying weed and feed in spring and autumn and then scarifying
4. Re-seeding a lawn or replacing patches with turf and re edging a lawn to give it back a strong definition
5. Pruning shrubs and small trees
6. Planting up pots and borders
7. Painting walls
8. Staining fences

Again, this list is not exhaustive but is the main bulk of a maintenance gardener work, especially weeding!!

Another area you could become involved in, is Garden Design.

This, when done properly, would require more specific training but is something you could incorporate into an initial working plan.

Garden Designer

A Garden Designer tends to be more of an ideas and creative person rather than a practical 'get your hands dirty' sort of person. Obviously, there are designers who would do the hard actual work, but on the whole they would be looking at:

1. Assessing the overall garden for all its aspects to improve
2. Looking at how a garden could be restructured, such as the shape of the lawn, the direction of a path, areas for borders
3. Looking at creating a totally new border of plants with colour or specific planting to create a certain mood in the garden
4. Looking at how a garden could be made to feel bigger through design or made to feel more secluded through design
5. Looking at how the practical requirements could be improved, such as where to store bins, where/how to store bikes, where best to put a greenhouse or shed

This is probably just scraping the surface of the tasks for a garden designer.

Another specific area you could be involved in, is becoming a Horticulturist.

Horticulturist

This is someone whose main focus is plants. They will likely have become an expert in this field. There are over 70,000 plants registered with the R.H.S, with new ones coming onto the market each year. So to have a wide knowledge base of that many plants takes some doing.

They will know exactly what plant will best suit what space in the garden, depending on factors such as soil type, aspects such as weather, shade or sun, the surrounding geography/topography and regional/seasonal variations.

They may grow and sell their own plants.

Finally, another specialized area of work would be, to become a tree surgeon.

Tree Surgeon

Someone who has had specific training to maintain the care of trees. Their tasks could include:

1. General care of tree through removal of dead branches.
2. Identifying diseases in a tree and identifying ways to treat the tree.
3. Seasonal pruning, such as 'crowing' in late Autumn/Winter (taking the top off a tree, giving it a hair cut)
4. Pollarding, which is a major prune of the top branches, to encourage growth of dense foliage and branches.
5. Removal of dead trees, including stump grinding.

Ok, let's come back to you and your skill base. When I was describing each definition, was there a category that you could see yourself fitting into more easily? Again, spend a few moments thinking of your work skills, your strengths and knowledge base.

Write down 5 skills you have, such as, I'm good at construction or I like to pay attention to detail. If you struggle with this exercise, ask a close friend or family member to suggest some skills they feel you have. You may be pleasantly surprised with what they say.

Ok, so in chapter 4 we have looked at the different type of areas where you could work in 'gardening'. We have looked at your skill base and how much pre knowledge and skills you may have, but what if having read this chapter you think you are lacking certain skills. The next chapter will look at the advantages of going for training. Or, do you need to undertake formal training in order to set up a good business?

To Train or Not to Train?

When I first thought of turning my hobby of gardening into a professional career, the thought of "I don't know enough" was strong. I am by nature, an academic, I like to learn. You may not be academic, more practical orientated. I will discuss both mind sets as you will see how both are useful.

Firstly, if the thought of "I don't know enough" is strong for you too, let me reassure you that you probably know more than you think, especially if you have been doing your own garden for a while.

Gardening, by nature, is a practical 'hands on' job, classed as non -skilled manual work. I would argue against it being 'non-skilled' as there is a certain amount of knowledge and skill you need to be a good professional worker. But, the majority of gardening is obvious and comes down to experience giving you the edge, like anything in life.

Advantages of R.H.S training

I chose to go to my local R.H.S Horticultural college in Cannington, to learn R.H.S Horticulture level 2 out of interest, before I'd even started gardening professionally. Once I was trading, I did Level 3.

For me, the training gave me a general overview of all aspects of gardening, that helped raise my confidence to be able to walk into any garden and have an idea of what needed doing.

The advantages of going to college were:

1. It was structured time, set aside to learn. Life is busy for everyone and sometimes it's hard to fit in everything we need to do, so picking up a book or browsing the internet in your own time can get put bottom of the list.

2. It provided great group peer support. You may love gardening but your nearest and dearest may not always want to hear the wonders of a gladioli or the fabulous new plant that you've discovered. So, being with like-minded people who are equally passionate and want to chat about gardening is invaluable. You can swop ideas of what would be a great plant to put where or how to overcome a certain problem.

3. Like I said, it raised my self-confidence to give me the confidence to go into any garden. Your customer may know their garden and plants inside out and be proud of what they have in their garden, even knowing the botanical names. To be able to be equally knowledgeable is a huge advantage. Your customer may be the complete opposite and have no clue. I have done many gardens where it was the deceased spouse who did the garden and the person remaining has no idea of what to do or no inclination. Which leads me to point 4.

4. Having done a formal R.H.S training course and be able to advertise that you are trained, gives the cus-

tomer confidence that you know what you're doing. It may be the difference between you getting your first job or not. If you do a good job and your customer is happy to recommend you, your business will thrive.

5. Having a formal qualification will help you register with a trading organisation that will recommend you, such as 'Checkatrade' or The Gardeners Guild and even shops and merchants, such as B+Q. There is no requirement to be registered with such organisations, but it may provide some initial jobs and give you a bit more kudos.

Advantages of experience alone

When I set up trading in 2012, I set up with a business partner who'd had no formal training but had experience, as it was his hobby. His experience and practical skills were just as valuable as any of my qualifications. What he didn't know, such as how to lay a patio, he looked up on the internet.

Today with so much information at our finger tips via the internet, you can easily be self-taught. There are apps such as Plant Snap which can identify plants for you from a photo taken on your phone.

You just need the discipline to put time aside to look up areas where you lack knowledge. And of course, the internet is a free resource. Which leads me to the next chapter which I'm sure is one that's upmost in your mind . . .all things financial.

Money Matters

The idea of money must surely have crossed your mind, from questions such as:

1. How much is it going to cost me to set up?
2. How much do I charge?
3. How do I charge?
4. How do I do a quote?
5. How much can I earn in a year?

These are some of the questions that raced through my mind at the beginning.

Ok, so start-up costs.

We have seen from Chapter 3 that you probably have enough basic tools already to start working, so what other outlay would there be?

Advertising

The first thing my partner and I did in the winter before we actually started gardening in the spring, was to set up a website and Facebook page. These were the basic skeleton structure, so that we had something to put 'out there' once we got going.

Obviously, the cost of a website will depend on factors such as how much detail you want on it, if you can set it up yourself or need to pay someone to do it for you. We will look at websites in more depth in chapter 7.

Facebook is obviously a free form of advertising and one that I highly recommend.

We will look further at different forms of advertising in the next chapter.

Insurance.

You need insurance.

You need Public Liability Insurance. This will cover you for things like, if you dig a hole and get called away by the customer and their nosey neighbour comes into the garden to see what you are doing, doesn't see the hole and falls down it.

I confess, I have cut through an electric cable that led to an outdoors lamp. Fortunately, I didn't electrocute myself as the owner had shut off the supply with the foresight that I might accidently cut through it.

Another example is, a young employee was strimming grass near a greenhouse and a stone flew up and smashed a pane of glass. Easily done.

On both occasions, the customers were kind and didn't get angry, but it could easily have gone the other way, which is why you need insurance.

Again, insurance quotes will depend on how much cover you need. But, to give you an idea, I am now a sole trader, with no employees, not doing anything too exciting like climbing heights or messing about in ponds. I have a basic cover. I have just renewed my P.L.I for £176 through Towergate Insurance. (cost price in 2020)

Waste Carriers License.

If you intend to remove garden greenery such as grass cuttings and weeds from a customer's garden and you are doing the right thing by taking this waste to your local recycling centre, you will need a Waste Carriers License.

The cost of this will vary according to how much waste you intend to take, how many times during the year and the nature of the waste. Organic matter, such as grass clippings and leaves will not cost as much as inorganic matter such as rubble and concrete.

Each council will charge differently, so you will need to check with your own council for its costings.

I have noticed my local recycling centre has got strict in the past few years about charging for commercial waste, so there is no avoiding it.

Other Licenses

If you are going to be using commercial chemical sprays for weed killing or Pesticides, you will need a license.

If you are going to be using a chainsaw, you need a license.

Contact the City and Guilds Ground Based Operator for various training options for both licenses.

Accountant

You may think why I have mentioned the need for an accountant, I'm in the early stages of a business, not earning much. In my experience, an accountant is worth every penny, pound or dollar. They will help you through the process of registering your business and help you with Self-Assessment for

HMRC. This is for paying Income Tax and Class 4 National Insurance Contributions.

A tax return needs to be completed by October if submitting a paper version or by January if submitting online. Any Tax owing is paid twice a year; it's split over payments in January and July. Tax is paid on your yearly profits once your 'personal allowance' has been accounted for. Personal allowance is the figure you can earn before you have to pay Tax. In 2020, personal allowance was £12,500.

Even after 20 years of being self-employed I still need to ask my accountant questions, especially as law changes.

For example, my accountant helped me with my application for the Small Business Grant that the U.K government offered during the Corona Virus in 2020.It was a simple process in the end, but it was a relief knowing I had done my Self- Assessment Tax returns for the past 3 years and my accountant had any information the government would have needed, if there had been a query.

You need to keep records of income and expenditure in order to complete your tax return. The best way is to keep a spread sheet. There is an example of one of my yearly spreadsheets in Appendix 1 at the back of the book. You are welcome to use it as the basis for one you create.

Across the top of the spreadsheet is each month, starting from your tax year (usually first week of April). Enter your incomings in each month. Down the side is a list all of your expenses/outgoings. Important to remember to keep all your receipts for expenses.

Each month, total up your expenses. Take the figure away from your incomings, to give you a rough idea of your profit or loss for each month. This spread sheet then becomes the basis for your Self -Assessment return. Or, if you use an accountant, you will send them a copy of this spreadsheet, for them to complete your return.

If you are disciplined to complete your spreadsheet every month, doing your tax return will be a lot easier at the end of the financial year.

There is an app called Quick Books, which may be worth looking into. It's an app that helps to organize your finances. It can scan receipts and keep them together in a file to assist in preparing yearly spreadsheet. It can prepare and track when invoices have been paid. It can prepare a tax return and check your VAT return for mistakes and much more. In 2020, it cost £20 a month

Your Fee

Ok, the nitty gritty question of "What do I charge"?

You have some options here.

You could charge an hourly rate, or a special half day/day rate. Or you could charge per job, rather than break it down. My advice for the early days would be to charge per hour. You need to establish in your own mind, how quick you work, how much you can physically get done in an hour. As you become more experienced, you will get quicker at the job.

To charge a flat price for the job works better if there is a team of you to get through the job quicker and you can fit 2 or 3 'big' jobs into a day.

The way my partner and I established how much to charge in the first year of trading, was to do a survey of as many local garden business as we could find. We phoned up to ask for a quote and asked how much per hour their charged. We had a range of charges, from £5 per hour to £20 per hour. This was in 2012. So we took the average cost and started at £15 per hour. We thought that was fair. Some people thought it was too expensive, but most were happy with that cost.

Skip to 2020, I now charge £20 per hour, which is cheap in my eyes, but I will explain why I don't feel I could charge more.

A business should increase its charge by 10% a year to keep up with inflation and increased costs from its source suppliers.

We made the mistake not to increase each year, as we thought we wouldn't want loads of small change rattling around. This was the times when people generally paid in cash. So we kept at a round figure of £15 for 7 years. If I'm honest, despite having a large customer base, we were apprehensive of putting up our fee, for fear of losing customers.

The inevitable happened.

Our additional 'unseen' costs all went up but we kept at our original fee. So things such as insurance, (we took on a young employee and the insurance quote rocketed) petrol, accountant fee, website retainment fee, replacement of tools (especially gloves and secateurs) annual service of mower, cost of plants and compost, delivery fees for large materials such as chippings. All these costs went up and we found ourselves working extra hard to maintain a reasonable income.

In fact, we had too many customers to comfortably handle; the downside of a success business. My head would be spinning with who we had done, who was next. Despite having a Monday morning plan of action to work out our plan of work, it was a mind field of balancing everyone. Throw in the great British weather, to completely throw any plans out of the window. We were both exhausted from long hours of work. Gardening is hard work when you are working solidly from 8.30am to 6.30pm. Which is why in Chapter 11 we will look at back care.

So, after a long discussion with my accountant, I decided to put my price up to £20. (I had gone sole trader at this point)

This felt like a huge jump from £15 to £20 for some people.

So, about a third of the customers left and found someone else. And, surprisingly, it was the best thing that could have happened.

Now I have a manageable amount of customers to comfortably fit in each day who are happy to pay.

Remember I said a business should increase its fee by 10% a year. So, I should, on that reckoning,7 years later be charging £25.50 per hour. Even if I had put my fee up by only £1 each year, 7 years down the line, the fee should be £22 per hour. So, at £20 I am still too cheap in comparison to the annual cost of living. Something for you to think on, to not make the same mistake.

Remember, as a self- employed person, you don't have the luxury of sick pay or holiday pay, if you don't work, you don't get paid. So make sure you set your rate of pay that will account for this.

Quotes and estimates

Have you ever had a new kitchen installed at home or needed a repair to your roof? I'm guessing you would have got 3 quotes to compare costings of different companies. This is sensible.

The same happens in gardening, especially the hard landscaping projects.

So, know that if someone phones you for a quote, the likely hood is that you are one on a list. This is nothing to be daunted by, but something to reassure you when you don't get a job, especially when you are keen to get new customers.

In my experience, quotes are tricky things to get right, because in gardening, there are many unforeseen situations which will alter a quote.

You generally don't know what is under the ground till you start digging. It's then that you come across lots of builders' rubble discreetly buried under a lawn or border, which takes extra effort, time and money to dig out and dispose of.

The job may take longer than planned because of weather conditions, such as heavy rain or snow delaying progress.

Materials, such as chippings may be out of stock and you have to wait for delivery.

The customer may change their mind what they want as the work progresses (This has happened for me) and you have a new plan of work to work to, which may involve additional costs for materials and your time. Obviously, this is not your fault, but is difficult to argue with a fixed quote.

Getting quotes right only comes with experience.

But a general rule of thumb is that quotes are provided freely to a customer. They are best written, in detail, as to what exactly your plan of work involves with costings for materials clearly outlined (include at least 10% to 15% mark up on the wholesale price)

Gardening always takes longer than you anticipate, so include an extra day to your quote, as contingency. If you don't need the day and you can give your customer a rebate, they will probably love it and put you in good favour. Much easier this, than to try to get extra money at the end of the job or having to 'take a hit' of a loss.

A customer has 14 days cooling off period to change their

mind if they don't wish to proceed.

In my view, for your early days of experience, it's best to give an estimate, not a quote. This makes it clear to account for those unforeseen circumstances and the customer cannot keep you to the fixed price of a quote, it gives you some ley way. Some customers will not like an estimate, but, honestly, there will always be plenty of other work to fill your time if the customer declines your services because you have provided an estimate rather than a quote.

Invoicing

Some customers may be using your services for their business premises, such as clearing the garden or car parking space for office buildings, clinics or Residential Homes.

It is professional to give an invoice to other business owners.

This should include your company name, your address, the customer address, the date the invoice is sent, the date the work was completed, how many hours work were completed at your hourly/day rate, the total amount of cost with details of how to pay, such as your bank details for a BACS transfer.

The customer has 30 days to pay an invoice, so don't always expect an immediate payment.

Advertising

"Can I have your business card please".

I have been asked this many times and I'm ashamed to say I no longer have one, but I gave out hundreds in the early days of my business.

You can easily spend a large sum of money on advertising, so let me take you through some of the forms of advertising and promotion that have worked best for me.

Some people still read physical newspapers. I have done a repeat credit card size advert in the back of my local paper and one off promotions in special feature editions, such as local events and gardening promotions.

I have done advert in promotional directories. For example, a paper directory that will be distributed through letterboxes.

I have done video promotion in G.P practice; the rolling video that plays in the corner of the waiting room.

I have done an advert on the back of G.P prescription cards.

All produced no interest.

The problem with such forms of advertising, is that you

need the person to repeatedly see the advert over weeks, especially newspaper adverts, which can add up to large sums of money.

Ok, let's look at other means of advertising.

1. **Paper flyers through peoples' doors.**
   This can be very time consuming, pounding the streets, pushing flyers through letterboxes. I got bit by a dog once. So just be aware of that potential danger. .Let's be brutally honest, most of the flyers and junk mail that are delivered to a house will more than likely go straight in the rubbish bin, or at best put in the recycling paper bin and never really get read or saved.

   There is a 1% return on this form of promotion. So you need to be pushing 100 flyers for 1 possibly interested customer.

   I live in a small village and put a flyer through all the homes, approximately 200 homes. I got 1 customer from it. That may not sound much, but that customer was a 90 years old gentleman who loved his garden but was physically unable to do it. He had a large garden and it resulted in 2 hours a week work over 6 years, before he sadly passed away. He was a really interesting man to chat to and I learnt a lot from him. So, the hours spent initially pushing all those redundant flyers through doors was worth it in the end.

2. **Vistaprint**
   Vistaprint are great for reasonable priced business cards and other forms of advertisement, such as per-

sonalized pens and magnetic banners that stick on the side of your car. This is ongoing advertisement where ever you take your car.

3. Free online Yell Listing.

In the U.K the old paper directory Yellow Pages, has deceased and is now an on line version. You can have a one lined entry with your business name and contact details, in the appropriate section, for free. I can't say this has produced much work, but I have had a few phone calls over the years from people asking for quotes.

4. Press Release.

I have done a self - written press release to be included in my local paper. This was a short summary promoting the service I offered when I was starting up. It created some amusement with friends and family.

The other form of promotion in the local paper I have used is to get my picture in the paper. My ex business partner and I created a colourful raised bed on a small boring patch of grass opposite our village Post Office (at the time). This produced a lot of interest as we worked on it, changing it through the seasons and it felt it was our contribution to our village, to brighten it up and create some floral interest. The local paper photographer came and took a photo of the 2 of us kneeling down next to the raised bed.

5. Local shop window and magazine advert.

This is a cheap and cheerful way of advertising. A small paper advert placed on my local post office shop 'Local Interest' board. It stays for months with a nominal cost and produces recognition.

Also, I have pinned my business card on the notice board at garden centres. This has produced a fair amount of work over the years. It did help that I use to work in my local garden centre during winter, so the owners knew me and could recommend me. It is worth getting to know the owners of a garden centre if there is one by you. Some may provide a discount if you trade with them.

I have also used the local community magazine that comes out 3 monthly, to advertise a credit card size advert. This is a magazine letting people know of up and coming events in the village, local clubs, such as W.I and local trades people. This has produced a lot of work over the years, as the older population in the village tend to keep the magazine and use it as a reference for local services. My village council charge £70 for a year worth of advertising. So you can see, it's a great form of advertising, as I have easily recouped that amount of outlay through the year.

6. Groups

I use to belong to my town R.H.S Horticulture group. I enjoyed attending this group as it was a group of fellow people passionate about gardening with a talk to educate and entertain .

The group has never had the pleasure of Monty Don visiting, yet.

The reason I mention this group is that my business partner and I represented the group at the first gardening challenge at the Royal Bath and West Show at Shepton Mallet. This is a huge local event, celebrating all things gardening and farming (there is likely to be such an event near you)

The challenge was to create a show garden from a bare patch of soil, using plants and hard landscaping products provided by the show, in 2 hours, which was quite tough going. We were against another couple next to us, with the exact same products and sized plot. Again, our photo was taken by the local newspaper with our contact details. Also, my R.H.S group put it in the monthly magazine.

7. **Plant sales/car boot sales**

I don't know if any other country has car boot sales, maybe American friends would have 'garage/yard sales'. To be honest car boot sales have faded in interest in the West Country, but may still be popular elsewhere in the U.K, so it's worth mentioning them. For years I grew plants and sold them at car boots sales. It was a lot of hard work, growing the plants, loading them in the car so they didn't get squashed, unloaded at the car boot and then reloading at the end. I never earned much money, but it got me known in my area.

Once a year, first weekend in May, I organized a popular plant sale in my village hall. In fact, I would hazard a guess that I'm most known in my village because of that yearly plant sale than actual gardening. I have also attended other events, such as flower shows and sold plants. Maybe you could do the same?

8. Talks

Ok, this may not be for everyone, as public speaking is top of the list for phobias, but if you can push through the unease and expand your comfort zone, then giving talks to local groups is a definite way to go. Groups will pay you to give a talk.Groups tend to have a list of recommended speakers and if you can get on that list, you will be speaking at many groups through the year. Ask if you can request a winter time talk, as this could be a means of income when you may not be gardening.

9. Website

It's probably fair to say that every business nowadays has a website. You need to be visible on line, there is no doubt of that. It is the present and future form of advertising, as paper adverts fade from existence.
There are many website designers now to use, it's a huge industry. You can however compile your own, as there are companies such
as WIX, Webdor and Go Daddy, which provide templates for you to use to create your own website. Potential customers will check up on your website to see your quality of work, price and recommendations, even before contacting you directly.

10. Social Media

Just like a website, having a presence on social media is a definite must.
I can honestly say, I have got loads of work from having a Facebook page, with lots of pictures of gardens

in the process to final end result and customer recommendations. Consider having a Twitter and Instagram account also.

Another form of social media advertising would be to do a Utube video or blog. I spend hours watching Utube gardening videos. They are a great back up for quick accessible knowledge on a range of topics.

"It's not what you know, but who you know".

Another form of social media advertising is to join networking groups such as Linkedin. This has become very popular in 2020, as due to the pandemic, we were restricted by how much we could actually travel, so socially connecting via technology has become essential. It gives a chance to expand your knowledge of people providing professional services (as discussed in chapter 2) and gives you an opportunity to give a talk on your services.

11. Word of Mouth Recommendation.

I have saved the best to last. In your early days of setting up and establishing a business, the people you actually know will be an invaluable source of potential work. You may choose to offer "mates rates" initially, but you never know who is watching you whilst you work and thinking they could also use your services. Your friends, family and exiting customers will know people you don't know, thereby expanding your potential customer base.

Ok, these 11 ideas of advertising were to get you thinking of ways you could promote yourself, maybe ways that are a bit 'outside of the box'.

Spend 10 minutes making 2 lists, one list of people you know who could be potential customers and one of other possible forms of advertising not mentioned above. For example, if you have children, maybe there are contacts, through meeting other parents at the school gate, for potential work or even offering, with the correct permission, to do gardening with your child and their school friends in the school setting. Let your imagination go free.

So, in this chapter, we have touched on different forms of advertising to get your name 'out there'. So what happens when the phone rings as a result of that advertising and you are asked if you are available to look at a garden? Gulp.

In the next chapter, we will look at the questions you need to be asking a customer on your first visit.

Initial Visit

Well done, you have your first customer. Are you feeling scared or excited, or both?

Over the years, you will be asked a lot if you could "just pop round and take a look at my garden". In my experience, no actual paid work comes from those visits. People want to pick your brains for ideas. So, best to tact fully decline.

But, you have a genuine interested potential customer who wants you to look at their garden with the view to hiring you.

What questions do you need to ask them?

You need to build rapport from the offset. Everyone likes praise and acknowledgement, so start by finding something in the garden that looks good, such as a lovely tree or shrub or the customers' choice of plants.

The first thing you need to establish, why are you there?

Is it for a one off landscaping project, a one off blitz of an overhaul/tidy up or regular visits for maintenance?

How did they get to know of you?

What is the garden space used for?

Is it for the family children to play in or the family dog to run around in?

Is it a space the customer spends a lot of time in?

What times of day do they spend in it? For example, they may be busy and have just an hour late evening to sit and unwind. This will influence where you place a seat for evening sun or where best to place pots.

How much time do they want to spend gardening themselves?

Get an idea of how knowledgeable the customer is and how interested they are in gardening and plants, as it will influence what level of discussion you have with them in the future.

Are they aiming for a "low maintenance garden"? Or, will you be the sole person to maintain the space?

Do they want a 'pretty garden to look at' or do they want the garden to be functional?

Do they like an informal 'cottage style' garden or do they prefer formality and structure?

Where do the bins and bikes live? Is there a shed, garage or greenhouse for storage?

Do they have a bin for garden waste that the council collect? Or will you be expected to remove garden waste?

Is there a washing line hole buried in the lawn? (need to be aware of running over any metal with a mower)

What direction does the sun travel through the garden?

Is it an exposed garden? Windy or sheltered? Overlooked by neighbours? with the customer looking to you for ideas to gain more privacy.

What's the soil condition like? Clay or sandy?

What colours does the customer like or hate?

What plants does the customer like or hate?

If it's a one off landscaping job, such as laying a patio, what budget does the customer have in mind?

What access to the garden is available? Is there a side entrance, or do you have to go through the house to get to the garden? Some customers are happy for you to have a key to the garage, gate or even house, but this usually comes once confidence and trust are established.

Is there a preferred day or time for your visits?

This is time for both parties to establish if they can work together, so be friendly, approachable and confident.

Remember, it's their garden, not yours, so always respect what the customer wants you to do, even if it's not what you would do in your own garden. I had to cut all the flower heads off a lavender in full bloom once, because the customer thought they took up too much space.

This respect for the customer brings to mind the known saying "the customer is always right". If you agree or not, bite your tongue!

This leads us on to the next chapter, to expand on what makes for good customer care.

Customer Care

You may be new to the idea of being self- employed.

Being self- employed is a different ball game than being employed by someone, because the success or failure of your business is solely in your hands. If you don't illicit good customer care, you don't have a viable business, so you have to get this aspect of business right.

A good rule of thumb is to treat the customer how you would want to be treated and always remember to COMMUNICATE well.

It starts from the initial phone call or enquiry

If you have listed a land line as your means of contact, the chances are you will be out of the house when they call. If they have left a message requesting a call back, make sure you do it as soon as you can. Nowadays, there is huge pressure on us to be available 27 hours a day 7 days a week, because technology has made it so. So, a customer will expect a prompt reply, especially if you are one of 2 or 3 other gardeners they have contacted.

The chances are, especially in summer, that you won't be home till 6/6.30pm. So expect to have to make calls in the evening, but have a cut-off point that sets a boundary, for you and customers. Customers know you will be at home in the evening and will call expecting you to answer. Establish that you are available to take calls say till 7pm and that the last call you make is 7.30pm.

One of the last questions to ask is "How did you get to know about me". Hopefully you are visiting this person through recommendation of an existing customer, or from one of your friends or family member. However, if this customer is from an unknown source, it's good to ask the question, as it will help establish where/how they became aware of you, in order for you to know the best means of where to invest in future advertising.

You may only list your mobile as your point of contact, which is ok, as the likelihood is that you will have your mobile with you all the time. However, if you are strimming or mowing, the noise may muffle the sound of the phone and you may not hear it, so when returning the call (ideally before moving onto your next customer), always apologize for having missed their call.

Memory. You need a good memory. People will like you to remember details you have talked about, even if it's the name of their cat or dog. As you build a rapport, it's important to remember details imparted to you, for example, their daughter is taking her exams next week, so that when you go back in 2, 3 or 4 weeks time you can ask politely how she did, it shows interest.

Time Keeping. Gardening can sometimes take longer than anticipated and planned for. The likely hood is that your customer base will be a lot of elderly customers. Some live alone and don't see anyone for days or weeks, so your visit is something that they look forward to. If you are going to be late, it's only polite to call the person to let them know.

Cards. A nice touch is to send a card (probably more to your elderly customers) for special occasions, such as their birthday, if you know it and definitely at Christmas.

Talking of Christmas, will you be working at this time of year? Gardening is a seasonal job, but there are still tasks you can do through the year to be working on your business. So, in the next chapter, we will look at a typical plan of work through the year.

Seasonal Plan of Work

When I first started gardening, there were some fairly fixed jobs to be done at specific times of the year. Nowadays, climate change has had a huge impact on the seasons and jobs are no longer fixed at certain times of the year. The year I wrote this book, the spring time in the U.K, the temperature in March, April and May was 20 to 25 degrees, which is more like the temperature you would expect in the warm summer months. June was rainy, which would have been more typical in April, a few years ago. I heard from a weather expert that he predicted wetter mild winter months, dry spring months and heavy rainy summer months. However, there is still a general rule of thumb to guide you. Let's look at each month and the sort of jobs you would expect to be doing. This isn't an exhaustive list of every job that needs doing, but is intended to give you an idea of the sort of work, in and outside of the garden, to undertake at which time of year. There are many books to give more specific detailed tasks to do in the garden. Take into account the climate of the area you live in and adjust accordingly.

January

Not a lot happening outside.

A great time to expand your knowledge base. You could read, watch T.V or Utube videos to learn more on a subject you feel a bit weak on, for example, identifying weeds or what plants to place in a dry deep shady area.

You could be getting your social media up to date or expanded.

A good time to go on holiday somewhere warm, as the chances are from March you will be busy.

Pay any tax owing and National Insurance Contribution.

You could be pruning trees this time of year.

February

Start getting prepared to return to work.

Make sure all your tools are clean and sharp. Get your mower, power tools and vehicle serviced.

It's not just your tools which need to be ready for work. Gardening is a physical job. Your body needs to be ready too. If you don't exercise through the dormant months and keep your physical strength and flexibility, you will suffer when you 'hit the road running' next month. So, start and maintain a daily exercise routine, including stretching, which we look at in detail in the next chapter.

If you haven't completed your account spread sheet each month, now is a good time to get on top of it.

Some jobs in the garden that can be done this time of year are:

Wisteria can be pruned hard to 2 buds.

Fruit trees can be planted and or pruned, but before new buds start to swell.

Bush and standard roses can be pruned.

Summer and Autumn flowering clematis can be pruned hard now

Onion, garlic and shallot sets can be planted.

Root cuttings of herbaceous perennial plants like phlox or Japanese anemones can be taken now.

March

The gardening year has started in earnest.

Now is the time to be planting seeds for plants for customers or yourself, or to sell to customers later in the year. Make use of inside conservatory space, south facing window sills or greenhouse space.

Once the weather starts to warm, you could be in customers' gardens digging over and mulching the borders and around shrubs. Mulching is the process of laying well rotted organic matter onto the soil. It could be leaf mulch, compost or bark based. Mulching does 2 things, it retains moisture in the soil (hence ideally to do this once the soil has warmed up and you aren't trapping frost into the soil) and reduces weeds from growing.

Winter flowering shrubs which have finished flowering, such as Viburnum, Dogwood and Heathers can be pruned back. Shrubs which flower on this years' growth should be cut back hard.

Ponds could be cleared out, but remember to keep any leaves or weed on the side for a couple of days to allow the insects to return to the water.

Depending on the temperature, you could start cutting lawns, on a high setting cut. Or laying turf to make new lawns or repairs to existing ones.

If its windy this month, it's a good idea to stake trees and tall shrubs. Supports for fast climbers such as clematis and honeysuckle could be installed now, including wires attached to walls.

First early potato seed tubers can be planted.

April

Early in April, plant Second early potato seed tubers.

Seed sown last month may be seedlings now, ready to 'pot on' to bigger pots.

You could start lawn care. Now is a good time to apply a weed and feed treatment that is high in nitrogen. And aerate the lawn (punching holes in the lawn by means of a machine or physically stabbing a fork into the lawn and applying a slight wiggle, to make a small hole. Then 2 weeks later, return to scarify. This is the process of removing moss and dead grass by raking out, either by hand with a metal wire sprung rake (a very strenuous job) or with a scarifying machine. The treatment needs to be a high content of nitrogen, specific for spring time, to encourage growth of new blades of grass. Don't apply an autumn treatment, as this is a higher content of potash (potassium) which is more designed to encourage strong root development, which is best for winter time when the top growth of grass will be dormant and you want to strengthen roots against harsh winter weather. You will be amazed at how much moss is removed. You also need to aerate the lawn, to encourage airflow of oxygen to the roots. You can do this by simply punching holes in the lawn by means of a machine or physically stabbing a fork in rows across the lawn and applying a slight wiggle to make a small hole. You could keep the moss to line hanging baskets next month. The lawn will look rough for a week or two whilst it recovers from this vigorous intervention, but it will benefit in the long term and be strong and healthy as a result. If there are a lot of gaps in the lawn after scarifying, you could add grass seed to the areas to bulk up the lawn. Ensure the seed is watered daily for at least a week to ensure germination. There may be worm casts at this time of year. These are plugs of soil that have been brought to the surface by worm activity. Simply break them down with a rake and rake into the lawn, the soil will not damage the lawn.

You could divide herbaceous perennials to make new plants for other areas of the garden.

Runner shoots from strawberries can be layered into the ground or into small pots.

You could be planting Evergreen shrubs.

Half- hardy annual plants can be sown.

Dead head tulips and daffodils but don't cut the leaves back, as the leaves are needed to feed the bulb. Cut the leaves when they are yellow. If leaves are cut back too soon, it will result in following years having weaker blooms to ultimately just leaves appearing but no flowers.

Main crop potato seed tubers can be sown now.

It's tempting for customers to want to start planting summer annuals, as they will start to appear in garden centres. But, discourage this, until the risk of frost is over, which is mid to late May. Patience now will definitely pay off.

May

You can be selling the plants you grew earlier, especially vegetable plants, which are ready to be planted out now into their final position.

Planting of summer annuals and or shrubs into pots or borders.

Dahlia tubers can be planted.

Once frosts have finished, hydrangeas can be hard pruned.

Lower the setting on your mower for a closer cut of lawns.

Wisteria can be tidied up by pruning to 5 buds.

Tie in grape vines.

Dead Head roses to encourage repeat flowering and remove dead diseased or crossing branches.

Remove the old flower heads of azaleas, rhododendrons and lilacs. Winter Heathers can have a light trim.

Hard prune of shrubs which flower in the spring on wood produced from the previous year, such as Forsythia.

The warmer weather and new growth may bring in insects such as aphids to plants such as roses and vegetables like beans, so removal by frothy washing up liquid water.

Ponds can be planted up.

Apply seed to lawns that need patches treating or just to thicken, once the area has been prepared by removing moss and roughing up the soil for seed to bed into. Water well and encourage the customer to water during dry weather.

Lots of weeding!

June

Greenhouses may be getting hot and any plants growing may need extra watering. Shading could be applied to the glass and water applied to the floor to dampen the air to keep the greenhouse cool.

You could pick any ripe fruit and vegetables growing in a garden, to give to less mobile customers.

Straw or other form of blanket protection placed under strawberries.

Side shoots from tomato plants are removed.

Shrubs that have finished flowering, such as Weigela can be pruned back hard. Flowering herbaceous perennials that have gone over can be cut off

Softwood cuttings of shrubs like lavender can be taken now.

Continue weeding.

If there has been a prolonged dry spell, raise the mower blade to prevent it scraping lawns.

July

Pay any Tax owing and National Insurance contribution.

Continue dead heading roses and cut back sucker shoots back to the base.

Strawberries should have finished now, so have a general tidy up and remove any old plants, to replace with baby plants from rooted runners.

Lateral growth of fruit trees, especially apple and pear, can be cut back to 5 leaves. Store hard fruit in a dry place. Apples should be stored so that they don't touch.

August

Fast growing hedges, for example laurel or privet will need a trim to keep their shape.

Summer is a good time to do layering propagation as the soil is warm and the new roots and shoots are more likely to grow. Also other cuttings, such as Pelargoniums will take well now.

Make sure climbers are kept tided in as there will be a lot of growth now.

Rambler roses that have finished flowering need a hard prune now, down to the base, with new shoots at the base being tied in to the formal structural support.

If it has been dry, the plants, especially roses, will need a good water. If roses get too dry at the roots, it makes them prone to mildew.

Summer time is a time that people will be away on holiday, so this is a time to offer a watering service.

September

Now is a good time to plant new shrubs and trees, as the soil is still warm to establish a strong root system going into the winter, but the sun is not so strong as in the summer to scorch new leaf growth.

This month is good to do Autumn lawn care. As you did in the Spring, apply a weed and feed fertilizer that has a high potassium content and then scarify. You could also apply seed this time of year as its still warm but more chance of rain onwards to establish strong roots.

Outdoor tomatoes and potatoes can be lifted now, with tomatoes being ripened inside now rather than outside and the healthy plant being put on a compost, as long as there's no blight.

October

This time of year is excellent for collecting loose leaves and storing in a black bin liner, to make leaf-mould. Fill a bag as much as possible, punch in holes at the base with your fork and fill with water. Store in a discreet place for 2 years for a great source of mulch or to dig the rotted organic matter into the soil as a soil improver.

Clear away the summer bedding, which will have finished now. Biennial plants, such as sweet Williams, can be planted now for flowering next year.

Plant bulbs for next spring.

Potatoes can be lifted now and stored for winter in a cool, dry and dark place.

November

We are coming towards the end of the gardening year. This is a time to start 'putting the garden to bed'. It's a time to clear and tidy the garden of dead leaves, removing any remaining plants that are dead or diseased.

Cut back deciduous hedges, such as beech and hawthorn.

Grapevines can be cut back to 2 buds.

Good time to give the borders a final mulch before the frosts start.

Towards the end of November, finish lawn cuts (although it may still be possible to cut lawns in December if it's a mild winter)

December

Put your feet up and enjoy a deserved rest, review your work from this year and dream of what you will be doing next year.

Self Care

In my view, this is probably the most important chapter of all.

To be self - employed is to be self -reliant and slightly selfish, as in, putting your health first above everything else. If you have a family and you feel responsible to take care of them, remember, if you are the sole income provider, if you don't work, you don't provide.

So your health is important. It can be stressful starting a new business venture, as there is so much to learn and establish, so keeping your stress levels down as much as possible will be essential. Remember to include time for your hobbies, even if that was gardening in your own garden before you took on looking after others gardens. You need a psychological outlet. You may find being out in the fresh air, breathing deeply, surrounded by nature and enjoying some quiet time for self - reflection whilst working alone helps to 'put the world to right'.

The main difference you will notice doing a physical job such as gardening, compared to an office based job, is the impact it has on your body. There's no denying it, you will be tired and achy after a full day of gardening.

The best way to keep aches and pains to a minimum

is good preparation and care of your muscles and joints, before you start work and at the end of the day.

I have found yoga to be invaluable. It is good to be physically strong, as you will be lifting heavy bags of compost, concrete mix and wooden sleepers when making raised beds. Also lifting the mower in and out of your vehicle repeatedly takes some strength, especially at the end of the day.

As good as it is to be physically strong, it is even more important to be flexible. You will be bending over, kneeling, crouching and reaching a lot in the day. Your lower back muscles, hamstring leg muscles and shoulder muscles need to be flexible.

A quick anatomy lesson for you now.

Muscles are made up of lots of thin fibers that flex and contract together synergistically as you move. They act a bit like rowers in a rowing boat, moving back and forth as you extend and retract your limbs. For example, when you reach out to pick up a cup, the inner muscles of your arm extend and the outer muscles contract. When you bring the cup to your mouth to drink, the inner muscles contract and the outer muscles extend. They work opposite each other but together. When the muscle fibers extend, they open up to allow in a fresh supply of oxygen filled blood, which helps the muscle to move. When the muscle fibers contract, they squeeze the fresh blood into the muscles and around the rest of the body. This helps to keep the muscles working well, but also clears out the 'rubbish' (toxins) from the blood that was in the muscle. Toxins are naturally produced through the breaking down of oxygen into usable components for the body.

If a muscle gets tight and inflexible, it's harder for the blood to flow through the fibers and so the toxins, especially lactic acid, get trapped in the fibers. This results in the stiff achy feeling that we feel, after a muscle has been worked. So, to keep the muscles flexible will result in less aches and pains the following day of a full day of gardening. How do you do that?

There are 2 things you must do and one thing I recommend you do every day.

You must stay hydrated, by drinking at least 6 pints of water. Muscles need water to stay lubricated and flexible. You will be sweating loads, especially during the summer months. If you don't keep your fluid levels up, it will likely result in headaches.

The second thing to do is daily stretches to your hamstring muscles, lower back muscles and shoulder muscles. You must do at least 10- 15 minutes of stretching your body before you start work and definitely at the end of your working day.

Stretches for your back

Child's Pose

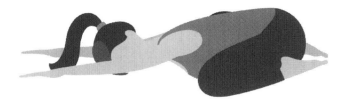

Cat Pose

Cow Pose

Downward Facing Dog

Half Lord of the Fishes

Spinal Twist

Stretches for your tummy, hip flexors and core muscles

Bharadvaja's twist

Boat Pose

Bound Angle Pose   Camel Pose

Lunge Pose

Stretches for your hamstring and glute muscles

Happy Baby Pose

Reclining hand to big toe Pose

Wide Angle Seated Forward Bend

Figure of 8 Pose

Stretches for your shoulders

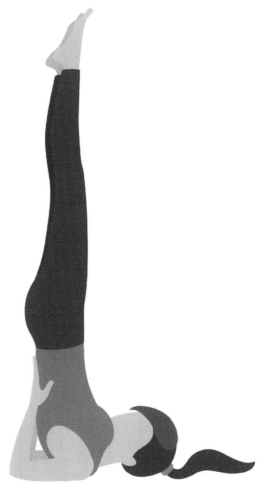

Shoulder stand

Deltoid stretch

Tricep stretch

These pictures are to give you an idea of the type of stretches you should be doing every day. It will probably be the last thing you want to do when you get home at the end of the day, but trust me, they are essential. I would advise never to over stretch a muscle. Get to know your muscles and know where your limits are when you stretch. Also, get to know a local osteopath, and go for a treatment on your body every so often, to keep your joints mobile.

One recommendation, is to either have a warm bath in the evening with added Epsom salts (approximately a large cup size worth of salts) or to take a supplement at night of Magnesium Sulfate. Magnesium Sulfate is Epsom salts, the same thing. Simplified, it is a mineral that naturally occurs in the body and works at night, at a cell level, to help clear the blood of toxins. This helps to relax the muscles. It results in less aches and pains in the morning and has definitely helped me.

As always, check with your G.P before taking any supplement, especially if you have blood pressure issues.

If you look after your body, you will be gardening for many years to come.

Ok, so we have looked at ways of how you can take care of your body and mind. You have control over that. Let's look, in the last chapter, of things that are out of your control, that may affect you and your business. These are things that may or may not seem obvious, but are worth taking consideration over.

A Last Note

In this last chapter, I want us to look at aspects involved in being a self – employed gardener that you may not had considered.

If you are reading this as a person who is the main income provider for yourself or your family and you are pondering if to change from a well-paid office based job to being a gardener, there is something you may need to be aware of and be prepared for; your family reaction to your decision.

People generally don't like change. We like normality and structure; this helps us feel safe. The Corona virus of 2020 tested our concepts of what is 'normal' and threw us into totally different ways of living. Some people found this stressful.

Your family have got a concept of you. They have known you for many years doing a certain job, which brings in a certain amount of income. Our work defines us, rightly or wrongly. When you meet someone for the first time, I bet one of the questions you ask them is "what do you do"? From that information, we construct an image of what their life is like, what their standard of living is etc.

Your family, no matter how supportive they are to you, will

need time to change their mental construct of the image they have of you and get use to a new person. You may have to reassure them that this new venture will be successful. You may be working different hours and days of the week than a previous job, such as returning home later than 5pm or working Saturdays, which may unsettle established family routines for a while. You may be taking holidays at a time of the year that seems unusual initially.

These may not be issues that you have to face, but it's something to be prepared for.

Knowing which plants to plant where is a challenge in the early days of gardening. I would suggest taking a walk around your neighbourhood and seeing which plants are growing in peoples' gardens. It will give you a guide as to what is deemed popular, but more importantly, it will show you which plants are happy to grow in your area. Get to know the geology of your area, such as, what the soil is like for PH levels and texture, the wind directions, if the garden is prone to frost pockets and if it prone to flooding. For example, I live on the coast. A mile in from the beach it is still light sandy soil, but 5 miles away, in my garden, it is heavy clay soil.

Keep learning about gardening. It's impossible to know everything; gardening is a life-long learning process. Just as you would expect a garden to develop, mature and change over years, the same applies to your knowledge, skill base and confidence as a gardener.

If you are working in the U.K, be prepared to change working plans according to the weather. You will become obsessed at watching the weather forecast. You may have a great plan of work for the week ahead, but the weather has other ideas. Learn to be flexible and adaptable. Also, out of courtesy, phone the customers you will not be able to visit. Most people will not expect you to work in heavy rain, but they will expect a call to rearrange your visit.

You will be working in peoples' personal space. A garden can be a special place and hold sentimental memories for people, such as where the family cat is buried or how their deceased spouse would spend hours in the garden. A garden can be a reflection of the person, their likes and dislikes, their creative expression and character. Be prepared to get to know your customer on a level that can be quite personal. Also, be prepared for a neighbor to politely enquire, over the garden fence, what you are doing in the garden. It may just be out of curiosity, but it may be because they are wondering if you could do work for them or someone they know.

Most people tend to pay by bank transfer online. You may need to remind people to do the transaction, as it's easy for them to get distracted and forget to do it. Also, it's not so instant as a customer paying you with cash at the end of your visit.

Be prepared to eat more biscuits than ever before. I hardly ate biscuits till I did the gardening work, but they are appreciated when you are working hard and burning off many calories. Be prepared for your body to change shape in the summer; invest in a good belt. Be sure to include plenty of protein in your diet, to maintain muscle structure, foods such as lean white meats (if you eat meat) nuts and pulses if vegetarian. Also include plenty of green leafy vegetables such as Kale, watercress, broccoli. It's great to know that you can indulge a little in sweet fatty foods over Christmas, knowing that it will easily be burnt off when the gardening work gets going in full swing. I have often joked with ladies who moan that they can't lose weight, that they are welcome to come and join me gardening, as the extra weight won't be a problem for them for long.

Conclusion

In conclusion, I would say there is no other job like gardening. In my view it is a great job, being outside in nature. It is rewarding to see tangible results from your efforts and know you are doing a job that people appreciate having done for them.

I would challenge you to be as much as organic gardener as much as possible. It's very easy to reach for the chemical sprays to quickly resolve a problem, but that only leads down the road to other issues, such as lack of natural predators and poor soil. We have seen the results of previous generations reliance on chemical intervention and we are paying the environmental cost for it now.

Nearly every person I know who is self-employed loves the freedom and sense of control it brings and would never want to be in full time employment via by an employer.

I hope this book has inspired you to go for it. Good luck in your new venture. I wish you many years of happy gardening and a successful blooming gardening business.

If I can be of any help with questions or queries, you can contact me on LinkedIn: https://www.linkedin.com/in/marie -glover-516a1624/r or I can be found on Facebook: https://www.facebook.com/mariegloverauthor/

Appendix

Tax Year						
Months		Jan	Feb	March		
						Total
Income		200	500	1000		1700
Outgoing						
Accountant		50	50	50		150
Tax		100	100	100		300
Website		200				200
Petrol		10	15	40		65
tools		50	300	45		395
Total		410	465	235		1110
profit +/-		-210	35	765		590

The above is the start of a typical spread sheet you would create for your accounts.

It includes:

Your business name

Your Tax year

The months of the year going horizontally across the spread sheet

Income for each month. Total up all your income and enter

the figure as total on the right side.

Your outgoings listed vertically on the left side and enter a total amount spent in each month for each category. For example, from the spread sheet above, I have spent a total of £50 on tools in January. Total up all your expenses in each month.

Take your total income figure, minus your expenses figure and you will calculate if you were in profit or loss for each month.

So, in the example above, you can see I had a total income in January of £200. I had a total spend in January of £410. So I made a loss in January of £210.

Doing the calculations of profit or loss for each month is purely for your information, to give you an idea of cash flow. It's probably not information your accountant, if you chose to hire one, will use for your final tax return. However, the main spread sheet figures will be used to prepare your final tax return. These figures need to tally with entries on your bank statement. So compile your monthly spread sheet figures from your bank statement.

About the Author

Marie Glover lives on the South West coast of England and one of her earliest happiest childhood memories is of playing in her grandparents' garden. In her adulthood she transformed that love into her own gardening business. She is also trained as an occupational therapist and enjoys a daily practice of yoga to help maintain physical flexibility and calm the mind.

Her garden is her sanctuary, which she shares with all forms of nature, especially her honeybee hives. She also enjoys singing in a ladies Barbershop group.

She is a lover of animals having had dogs, rabbit, and Guinea pigs share her home. She loves travelling to see other cultures architecture and trying different foods.

Connect with Marie here:
Facebook:
https://www.facebook.com/mariegloverauthor/
LinkedIn
https://www.linkedin.com/in/marie-glover-516a1624/

Printed in Great Britain
by Amazon